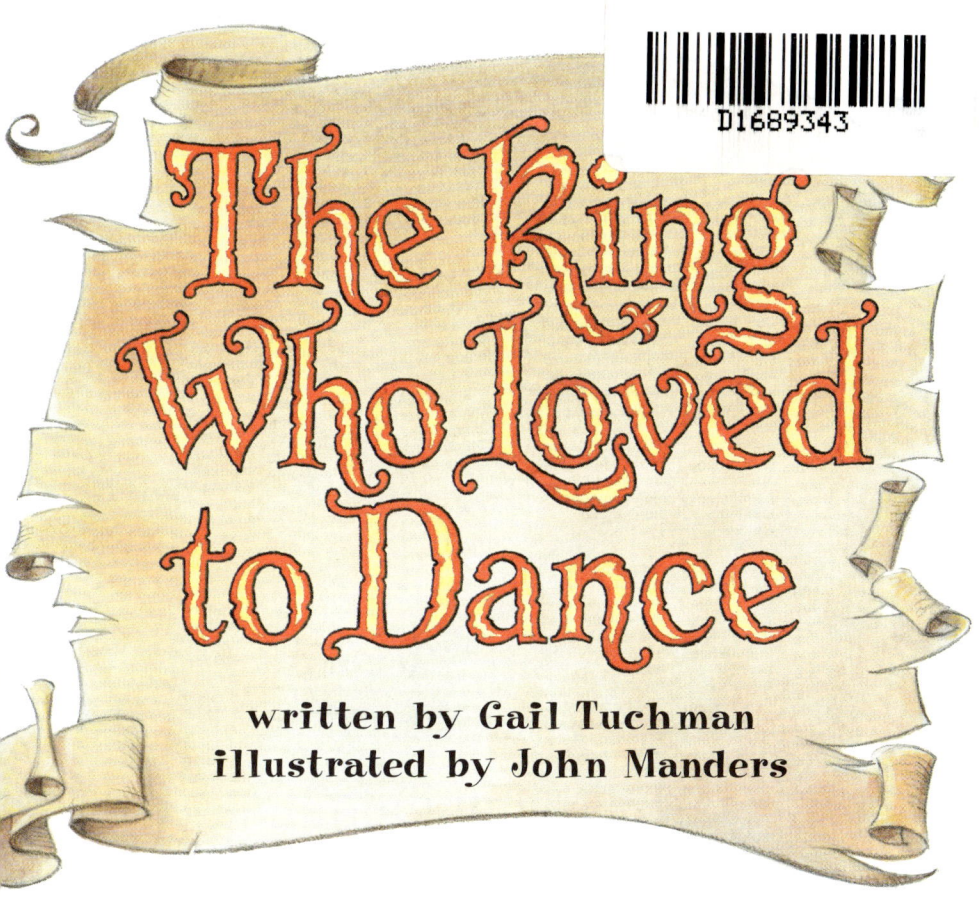

The King Who Loved to Dance

written by Gail Tuchman
illustrated by John Manders

HARCOURT BRACE & COMPANY

Orlando Atlanta Austin Boston San Francisco Chicago Dallas New York
Toronto London

The king danced to a singer's song — dancing, dancing, all day long. He danced outside and into town — dancing, dancing, all around.

He danced down a rocky slope —
dancing, dancing, with a rope.

Then the king's singer went away.
And the king sadly sat all day.
Everyone knew what was wrong.
The king couldn't dance without a song.
So —

The cows mooed, the horses neighed,
The bees buzzed, the donkeys brayed.
The king danced to their song —
dancing, dancing all day long.